In memory of my mother

'Some griefs build the soul a spacious house'
Edith Wharton, *The Touchstone* (1900)

The Heron on the Lake

Jean Andrews

Published 2015 by arima publishing

www.arimapublishing.com

ISBN 978 1 84549 660 9

© Jean Andrews 2015

All rights reserved

This book is copyright. Subject to statutory exception and to provisions of relevant collective licensing agreements, no part of this publication may be reproduced, stored in a retrieval system, or transmitted in any form or by any means, without the prior written permission of the author.

Printed and bound in the United Kingdom

This book is sold subject to the conditions that it shall not, by way of trade or otherwise, be lent, re-sold, hired out, or otherwise circulated without the publisher's prior consent in any form of binding or cover other than that which it is published and without a similar condition including this condition being imposed on the subsequent purchaser.

arima publishing
ASK House, Northgate Avenue
Bury St Edmunds, Suffolk IP32 6BB
t: (+44) 01284 700321

www.arimapublishing.com

Acknowledgements

'The Moon in Darkness' appeared in *Crannóg*, "One of Nature's Gentlemen' in *West 47*, 'Two Worlds' and 'West' in *Gentle Reader Poetry*, 'Bologna' (as 'Planes') in *Poetry Monthly*, 'Lipoczi', 'Easter Monday', 'Ventilation' and 'At Peace' (as 'Uncle') in *The Galway Review*.

'Bloc' appeared in *SPLAT*, the in-house review of the Department of Spanish, Portuguese and Latin American Studies at the University of Nottingham. I would like to thank my colleagues for their kindness towards my poetic endeavours.

I would also like to thank Máire Holmes and Lorna Shaughnessy for their constant support.

Contents

West	7
Two Worlds	9
Café A Brasileira	10
In October	11
Bologna	12
Knife's Edge	14
The Moon in Darkness	15
That Tree	16
Lightning	17
Drake	18
Downpour	19
The Short Sweep	21
Petunias	23
One of Nature's Gentlemen	24
Another Tree	25
The Taliban	26
Wollaton Hall	27
The Heron on the Lake	28
The Cat-Flap Again	29

Insomnia	30
The Gun Club Minute-Book	31
Eau-de-Nil Sky	32
Sanctuary	33
For Sale	34
The Fort	35
Ventilation	37
Long	38
Brolly	39
Long 2	40
Longer Ago	41
The Ship Once More	42
As To Where The Blood And Guts Are	43
Lipoczi	44
Salthill, 1980	45
Der Tod und das Mädchen	46
My Menagerie	47
Seventy-Four	48
At Peace	49
Hope Chest	51
April Fool's Day	52
The Tennessee Waltz	53
Flanders	55
Easter Monday	56

Sic transit	58
Pabellón del Espejo	60
Arrest	61
Good Friday	62
Mooghaun	63
Insomnia 2	64
Sheringham	65
Carmen	66
Armistice (1918)	67
Useless	68
Long 3	69
The End	70
The Heron on the Lake 2	71
Mili-	72
Account Closed	73
The Old Home	74
Honeymoon	75
The Fit	77
Bloc	78
The Heron on the Lake 3	79
Epilogue: Easter Saturday	80

West

West with the sunset
lies what is gone.
A world of old people,
old sayings, old ways,
memories with none to remember them,
the black bread, cocoa instead of tea,
meat in ounces, eggs in ones or twos,
compulsory tillage and coupons for anything
you couldn't grow yourself.
And these were good years
for the war never came.

Then, there were jet-planes
and film stars passing through,
but you couldn't go to a friend's funeral
if she was a Protestant.
You huddled with the rest on the church threshold
and that was daring too.
Confraternities and climbing Croagh Patrick,
the pictures, dances you cycled to
and back from, unmolested
if the men were gentlemen,
though that was once not the case
and you never forgot.

This you did
while mourning a mother
too fiercely loved
for easy surrender.
But children and home
finally came,
a realm of your own
to rule over and savour.
After so little affection, so much.
The sixties passed and the next decades flew.
What did politics or violent change matter?
The inner world was enough.

Then a loss too cruel for contemplation,
twice in one lifetime,
and the old nightmare started again.
This time you opted to wait
for the axeman to come to you.

Two Worlds

Two worlds
side by side,
one for the dead,
the other the alive.

A grave growing daffodils,
roses and antirrhinums
lying eastward
on the breast of a hill,
aeroplanes in arabesques overhead
and the acrid, sweet smell
of dung.

Two corpses together,
heads tilted down towards the sunset,
fabric and bone,
a road glistening below,
bullocks idling in the fields,
and family life going on
in the houses beyond.

Two worlds:
the living,
and the dead and gone.

Café A Brasileira, Lisbon

The last time I was here
I thought the universe had put in place
someone to catch me,
planning for bereavement
at breakneck pace.

Yet, when the moment came
for me to step up to the plate,
there was nobody and nothing
waiting offstage.

In October

An old lady
who had lived
among half-jumbled dreams
for a decade short of a century
lay on her hospital bed and asked:
'am I not dead yet?'
and 'have they started the war
in Afghanistan?'

She never missed a beat,
though everyone said
she had long since
been adrift with the fairies.

When she was younger,
she wore gaudy, beautiful things,
like a princess of Byzantium,
and cherished all of these
in her fogbound years,
hemmed in a room too tight
for her treasures and memories,
– a hope chest of elfin threads
and tatterdemalion fantasies.

Bologna

We all have something to say
about the Twin Towers.
For a long time, I thought it would be
disrespectful and self-indulgent
to offer any utterance to my tiny experience.
I never saw them, never set foot on American soil,
don't know what it's like to live through a war,
to be prepared to fight and wager everything
because there's no alternative.

I do know what it is
to be taken unawares by loss.

We all saw the pictures.
I saw them later than most
and not in the comfort of my own home.
I heard it in another language,
read it in a foreign press,
one more open and more volatile,
less circumspect than ours.
The keyword in those after-hours
and days and weeks
was *paura*, fear.

As luck would have it,
I was in a city of famous towers,
terracotta giants leaning into each other
like long-term lovers with juicy secrets,
the whole a monument to all the best
European humanism and civilisation could provide.
There was a political assassination there,
not far away, not two months later,
around the time that other New York plane,
Santo Domingo-bound,
came down.

I think it all affected my one remaining parent.
She dropped me, barely-formed,
into the Cuban Missile crisis
and took her leave
as bombs rained down on Kandahar,
not a month into that quasi-primeval,
asymmetric free-for all.
She had lived for family
and in the present moment,
but baulked at the immediacy
of a far-flung war.

Knife's Edge

The fall of a house of cards
can slice through flesh like a blade.
A precipice once danced upon
as if it had
all the amplitude
of a Belle Époque ballroom.

The Moon in Darkness

Things I would have wanted you to see:
the moon in darkness over the water,
the islands almost too flat for the eye to see,
the single seagull tiptoeing, prissy, in the breakers,
the Castrol GTX cap marooned in a puddle on the
    rocks,
a cow of Isis grazing, knee-deep and camera-happy,
    in a ditch,
water-logged blackberries demure by the side of a
    road,
the same road a boreen with blasted crag all round,
and a panorama across the ocean to Clare.

This, and much unsaid,
I have to declare.

That Tree

All those gambits which had worked before,
at other times, in different places,
could not get you to look at that tree.

That gracious macrocarpa,
cobwebbed in black and charcoal and green,
on a day which might have been – polarised –
on a backlit HDi flatscreen.

In retrospect, it seems to me
that this old being, in all its plangent majesty,
deserved much more from you, by way of salutation,
than cranky, ill-at-ease contumely
and squirming fabrication.

Lightning

We stood together but apart,
underneath the arch
of an eighteenth-century masterpiece
with enough glass
to make it transparent,
a place of worship
held up
by a skeleton of stone;
jagged veins of lightning
ripping through the clouds,
and our earthbound constellation
traumatised and out of sorts.

Drake

I will never expel from my mind
that copper-headed duck
minding his own business
on a busy lake
one Sunday
in St James' Park.

An afternoon
when a donkey and an armadillo
walked across the water
to take you by the hand,
to take you, indeed,
off my hands,
away to find
the hiding-places
of the heart.

Downpour

Lightning split the sky,
a sky so pale
you could barely see the threadveins
in the parchment
up on high.

Sheltered
by the smooth stone arch
of a regency church,
we watched the uproar from a dry patch
on the other side of the street.

A row of townhouses,
Georgian, bevelled and neat,
paint-chipped, fragile attics
level with the tops of the trees,
mice, or tiny servants mayhap,
cowering there,
spectres trembling in the eaves.

Once, my father would launch us
into fields
to square our shoulders
at the thunder.
No child of his would be afraid
amid the majesty of Nature.

At home, his wife
turned mirrors to the wall
in terror at the savage conflagration.
She would have scrambled underneath their bed
and given in to atavistic inclination
could she have faced the gossip of her neighbours
in stern concatenation.

While all the time
that showman she had wed
proclaimed,
in devilment and jubilation,
that this was just the barrels
bouncing down
from off the lorry overhead:
the porter being unloaded
at the public houses
of the dear departed, thirsty dead.

The Short Sweep

I'd caught the sun on my cheekbones.
You noticed
when I collected you from the train.

It happened on the short sweep
at the point where a raised boreen
makes a causeway through the bog.
It smells of clover and ragwort and turf
and the mudland can flood in winter
cutting the lower fields off.

Now, a group of placid Friesians swat their tails,
drop sweet-and-sour pats on the reedy grass
and the children play in the dappled patterns
thrown by the midsummer blossom and their hearts.

Then, along the road, between the trees,
there were ominous, ramshackle shebeens
with dogs we ran from as children
and gruesome old codgers and hags
who might steal our future away
to an end far darker
than our nightmares could conceive.

But once I walked this road,
in twilight, with my father,
myself not too long removed
from our infant abode
above the clouds.

My brother, though younger,
yet fearful or weary,
asked on repeated occasions
had we still much further to go,
but I heard the sounds
of the night-sky constellations
and knew we were never
that far from home.

Petunias

Nearly the end of May
and late to start them,
but I planted petunias today.

'Cheerleader Sunburst'
in green plastic pots,
with, I'm sorry to say,
the wrong type of compost.

They don't know it yet,
that it's not the most appropriate blend
for their nutritional needs.
Maybe if I don't let on
they won't take any heed.

I also polished the silver
and the avuncular brass.
My mother did them every two weeks.

I put my father's cuttings in a folder,
snippets from the prizes that he won,
a long time ago, before I was born.

It was more or less a must,
now the '50s newsprint
is crumbling to dust.

One of Nature's Gentlemen

A man may leave his seed and breed behind him
like a cuckoo, in another man's nest,
pass on, unacknowledged,
his manifold gifts,
which, in another realm,
would have come to fruition
under his own name,
instead of spending everything
on the roadside of contentment,
too diffident to complain,
showering those who listened
with a softly maddened wisdom,
otherwise scattering it to the rain.

Another Tree

For a long time after she died
I was afraid of a tree three gardens removed from
    ours.
There was one just like it, maybe a garden and a half
    away
and the same pair of magpies sat in both, in rotation,
but whatever it was, at dusk, in mounting dark,
that one did not pull me in with its swirling, leaden
    invitation.

I used to sit there in the gloom staring it down,
clutching at my terror as it faded to pitch black,
and twilight, which had always been a friend to me,
full of dreamy, flitting pleasures,
became, for months on end, a quagmire
beyond all footfall, rhyme or measure.

The Taliban

I told the doctor once
the Taliban were coming in the cat-flap
at four in the morning,
when the war and my insomnia
were at their height,
when she lay suffocating
on a ventilator,
fighting her last fight.

I had enough perspective at the time
to know it was amusing,
to think it might alleviate his day,
since there was nothing
either he or I could do
to change the course of mine.

Wollaton Hall

For Jane-Marie

Balanced on grief as on a scimitar-blade
with the cold sun of winter on the lake,
the russet tones of the Elizabethan sandstone
    blanched
and the afternoon closing in towards fearsome dark,
I tried some tentative steps back
to everyday, tangible ways.

The channels to the other world are always open,
the cave-mouth gapes at each and every corner,
the trick is to ignore that lurking danger,
in every tree, in every incline, every valley in this
    park,
and wait for plain and ordinary things
to reel you steadily back in,
'til all is cork-lined,
impervious once more.

The Heron on the Lake

Reasons to stay:
the heron on the lake
outside the Binnenhof
in the Hague.

I got so very close to death,
went with her every step of the way
until my legs grew heavy and ponderous
as if they were wading through solid seas of clay.

Then, when she was dead,
it seemed more logical to carry on,
a journey I would finish, in any case,
some other day.

But they were there,
the reasons to remain:
the heron on the lake,
the hope of love when I had none

and furthermore,
the things that I might say
with one foot in the grave,
and eyes bereft of scales.

The Cat-Flap Again

The toadstools came in last night.
After all this time they gave me a fright,
with their pinchbeck snouts
and their parchmenty, gill-lined sombreros,
their stiff-jointed dance to a faldelolero.

Denizens they had been of my long secuestration
in the sylvan harem of sleep deprivation,
those palimpsestic scenes from Dadd and Grimm,
jerking the lips of their moues,
pricking their puckered-up grins.

I said enough –
you vile creatures of the absent light,
desist!

And, in fairness to them,
they threw in the sponge
and scuttled right back
to their bunkers.
You'll find them today,
impassive and glum,
and squatting, stock-still,
on their hunkers.

Insomnia

I can't stop sleeping now
and, no, since you ask,
it's not from depression,
it's more like a boom
that has finally come
after deep, all-pervading
recession.

The Gun Club Minute-Book

A book bought
but hardly written in,
pages touched, maybe glanced off,
by your hand
before you ever had a thought
of not being here
anymore.

Now that I am come back
to common ways,
those things that insulate
and keep us safe,
if I must have a justification
it will be this book.
In it, I will write across your silence.
I will take my place at the gatepost
and keep an eye,
in this time of healing,
on the passers-by
and those passing through.

Eau-de-Nil Sky

Cotton-wool balls and a pink-tinged, eau-de-Nil sky,
the sea below, gunmetal high,
a plane in-between descending to land
and postscripts now to be etched in the sand.

The slumbered awake to another day's chores,
their cars on the drives, their cereal bowls,
the national news and an incoming Low,
the journey: a bare hundred miles yet to go.

My West awaits, and a mending too,
where the hymeneal must patch and make do
in blending their grief with new-minted passion;
and those left behind, on a much smaller ration.

Sanctuary

Find me sanctuary,
just for a year or two.
Let me back into the old certainties
without a thought for the immanence
of the other side.

Let me walk the road taken,
the path severally crossed,
crush twigs, already broken,
with the soles of my feet,
stand in other people's shoes.

Just for a while,
until I have the strength I used to have
when I knew death to be for others
and the extremities of this mortal life
copper-bottomed and intact.

For Sale

All the drawers are empty now,
her bed is in a different place,
my dolls have emigrated in a strong plastic bag
and her mound is sinking into the grave.

An eternal soul almost a whole year gone
and the house where I was conceived and born is up
    for sale,
the by-pass she swore she would never see is partly
    done
and no-one is sure how the village will alter in its
    wake.

On the hill, her tomb earth is bald and cold,
littered with felspar, detritus and stones,
grass, like a doll's scalp, sparse on the fresh-buried
    bones,
for there is no-one to see now to the weeds, the
    lichen, the flowers
and strangers have been prevailed upon to gravel off
that square of hallowed ground she tended for a
    widowhood
of thirteen years, five months, some weeks
and all throughout those spellbound final hours.

The Fort

The land this time last year
was all that was left to me.
I looked north and south and east
and watched the watery sun go down
in December
along the silver mud of the estuary
and the lands of perfect love
that lie beyond it,
out where the lost ones sleep
or keep an eternal peace
in the Westerly realm
of the beautiful, ever-young.

The North stood perpetual,
austere and demanding,
a place of hazel wands stripped bare,
all squinting in the wind,
familiar, but
no comfort there,
no balm of relief.
The South, a contrast,
explosive and warm,
crackling the fire
of walks and jokes and stories past,
a haven for always,
and yes, fuel to reboot.
Leaving the East,
far distant, beyond the pale,
an outland with no maps,
nebulous, insistent,
the least secure of all the paths.

I took it nonetheless.
And here I am,
a year has gone,
returned to exile,
navigating,
hanging on.

Ventilation

My mother's was the kind of world
in which something was always to blame.
So when it came to dying,
without a thought
she pinned it on us,
swearing we made her climb a huge great tree
when she should have been on her sickbed
and kept her there until she was all out of breath
and the only possible conclusion
was early, untimely death;
that we put her on a patch of green lawn
and made her run on the spot
and jump about until her insides burst
and she fell down
and down into unconsciousness.
She'd change the lock
on the front door when she got better
and that'd fix us,
she said.

*Long**

In the arms of a dancer
my ship came in.
Whether I will be allowed on board
is a question I can not answer,
she is still afloat
and I remain
thunderstruck
on the shore.

* *Long* is the Gaelic word for ship

Brolly

It was sullen and dreek.
The rain like hollow tubes of perspex
pierced by the on-rushing cars,
smudging the lines in the dark.
Your trend-cool blue brolly from Muji,
my men's black one, more ordinary,
like Seurat figurines
gliding across
somewhere between Habitat and Heal's,
dripping moisture on new-laid furniture-shop floors,
laughing and testing stealth-bomber runners in
    drawers,
breathing the beeswax, coffee, patchouli airs.
You sought a lounger to fall asleep in before the TV,
one incongruous, naturally,
in a rest home
or beneath the seated, pin-stripe trousers
of a chairman of the board.

You didn't find it.
So you took flight with the Muji
in a taxi,
pristine white,
with its rear lights winking in the rain;
bob-tailed, gorgeous,
geometric, mundane,
a hackney to your debut home
and attic habitation.

Long 2

The ship has docked a few times now
and I have been aboard.
When I am there nothing matters
but the intensity of the moment.
When I am ashore again
the same thing is constant torment.

Longer Ago

When he lay dying
I thought there would be love at the end,
an equal but a different one
to occupy a new and separate space;
I did not foresee the long pilgrimage
into aloneness and self-sufficiency
which would be its reverse face.

The Ship Once More

And so, can we be friends?
Yes,
but that won't stop us
tumbling into something else –

the ship has docked
and both of us have gone aboard,
with caveats. Indeed,
only the ship knows it course –

in seven years, it might come again
like the Flying Dutchman,
though what we'll be by then
is anybody's guess.

As To Where The Blood And Guts Are

If I camp out for long enough
on the mountains of Despair
nothing will matter,
certainly not holding on to life.

Once into monochrome
the footholds lurch away,
dissolving underfoot
like ink washed from a page.

In the vacuum:
a rusty iron bell-weight
and a constant nausea
of disorientation.

The only thing is to endure
like a pack animal,
until some freak of fate
jerks the lights back on.

Lipoczi

Lipoczi,
an alien name
in a Church of Ireland graveyard,
in the walled, portcullised portion
at the back of the church.

Shouldn't it be with the Catholic brethern
on the sunny slope at the front?
He was a Polish Second World War pilot,
after all?

But Iris was the wife of Lipoczi
and she had the right to be buried there
even if her workmates couldn't come in for the
    funeral,
but huddled on the steps instead,
furtive, grieving, defiant,
half in, half beyond
obeisance.

My grandparents lie behind the lych gate
and my uncles who died before the First World War,
also my aunt, their sister,
who lived to see the American bombardment of
    Kandahar.

Oh, and my mother was one who mourned from the
    threshold
with her comrades, all those years before.

Salthill, 1980

All those years ago,
walking along Salthill Road,
amazed by the trees outside the Jes
or the modular, white-faced apartments opposite,
or the lucid smell of the sea
or the fact that Protestant and Catholic
lived side by side,
in indistinguishable poverty,
in the little houses of the Claddagh.

The whole world was exotic
and full of experience.
I yearned for facts and knowledge,
swallowed them up like a goldfish
though I had no idea what to say back then;
about them or any other epiphanic thing.

I spent years looking for the answer
– you can imagine –
until, in the end, frustrated, it confronted me.
It said I should give up all that malarkey
and simply trust what I could touch, hear, see.

Of course, the word 'simply' turned out to be
a lot more trouble
than any of the other three.

Der Tod und das Mädchen

> i.m. Ingeborgh Bachmann
> (1926-1973)

I did not know until a day or so ago
that you had died of injuries
sustained in a house fire in Rome.

And you had not seen your half century in
when you died.

Yet all the while spoke obsessively
of your own death.

Did it come to you then
as a great surprise?

Was the fire an unwelcome intruder
on well-laid plans and time, cherished in
    anticipation?

Were you robbed or did you acquiesce
and welcome in the flame-clad stranger?

Was it time to let him take you to that bed
where, in his arms, you would do nothing more than
    sleep?

My Menagerie

Mary I was given when I was four,
Susie, I don't remember,
maybe a year before,
and then I cut off all her hair.
Years later, when I was ten,
I asked for Sally with her flowing locks,
but her blonde mane looked more like candy floss.

She's the least well made of all
and now has a limb which won't stay on,
my token disabled one, I suppose.
I kept them all in bed in a drawer for years,
with a threadbare, darn-eared, khaki-furred bear,
Teddy, a bastion of his kind.

These days, they're all set out on a rattan chest,
jumbled together with more recent arrivals,
a latter-day forest of furry friends.
Mary gives what might be a fascist salute,
but regally, and with the left hand.
Clothed in knitted blue, she keeps them all
in ladylike order, à la *Woman and Home*
circa nineteen sixty four.

I once remembered so much more
about the origins of each
but now there's no-one who can set me right.
If I misplace an incident or two,
we're on our own with the past;
no doll, bear, human of us
able to corroborate the facts.

Seventy-Four

My mother would have been seventy-four today.
I see now it would have been a step too far,
her essence was strong, her carapace weak.
She would have shied at being tethered
to the kindness of the young.

Notwithstanding,
I assured her for years she would reach
at least seventy-eight,
like her grandfather
who drank them out of a farm, a pub and a shop
and was found dead working in the fields
at that gallant and venerable age,
taken as if by accident or surprise
and still, in his own mind, a farmer in his prime.

At Peace

I saw him,
younger than I would ever have known him,
in a duck-egg blue, lambswool, v-neck pullover,
slimmer and cleaner of line, hair and moustache
than in my lifetime,
and happier, more open,
alive to a future, perhaps,
before it never happened,
became ossified in irretrievable past,
before he turned into an old cove
in tweed jacket and too many fags,
in a one-room bedsit
with a poster of topless Samantha Fox
on a cupboard masquerading
as a kitchen for a mature, then elderly, man,
trading on a store of jaunty escapades
assembled in an annual fortnight's
grouse moor, Scotch and pub-grub charabanc.

Now in his grave on a bleak hillside,
two decades and more in timber and fabric and bone,
there are hardly any left who remember him.
The tombstone, at his request, reads 'At Peace'
though most of his life was spent
a long, long way from home.

And yet, this once he brought himself to mind,
safe-conduct from the shadows
one single time:
delivery of a bashful legacy -
bendicite,
from one who proved, to all attempts, hermetic,
cowled and unpropagated, while alive.

Hope Chest

Every Valentine's Eve
she still hoped
that this year
the roses would knock on her
dilapidated door.
Attrition and solitude
had not utterly withered the desire
to be, once more,
the recipient of thorn-free, long-stemmed
symmetrical blooms,
with declaration card and sateen bows,
bearing as much relation
to a garden rose
as their cellophane shroud
to a kiss.

April Fool's Day

'My handwriting goes up and down'
and, in that, you should be able to tell
the traits of my personality.
We all like to hear about ourselves –
the good things, anyway.

The Tennessee Waltz

The first year passed in an agony of anticipation,
    endless silence,
rendered minor by other, overwhelming grief.
The second was brought to a close
by coffee cups like flying saucers on the terrace in
    Russell Square,
your latest announcement, our orbits flying apart,
but I held in there,
for another year
which ended, after much peregrination,
with Summer clouds
and a downpour at the Lace Market church of St
    Mary's.
Then back to silence with one reprieve:
a copper-headed duck in the Autumn,
on the lake, from a bench, in St James's Park.

By Christmas, the golden dome over the pulpit in St
    Mark's,
the piazza on a winter's night with stars,
a waltz to no music, shoes which left no space for
    mine,
all that azure beauty in the city I had dreamt of all
    my life,
those swooning canals,
all on the understanding, as you said,
that you had been no more than a figment of a futile
    imagination
and I had brought it all upon myself.

And now?
The memory of a rolling park
and a double doorway in a neo-Palladian country
    house.
You in that setting,
for a second year, for the second time,
vaguely unkempt, in turquoise and blue,
a black blister on the sole of one of your creamy feet,
a waltz and a walk in Elysian Fields.

All that distance,
all that intensity
defines what is lost,
that and the Tennessee Waltz.

Flanders

My father always said
if he'd been born in England
he'd have been pushing up poppies in Flanders,
instead of dying peacefully in a hospital bed.

He'd mixed up the two World Wars.
Even so, more than enough said.

Easter Monday

You take tiny little petal steps now,
thousands of them every day.
You can't trust the world anymore
so you must be always wary of attack,
especially from those who say they care, because
they change shape, almost all the time,
and new faces lie, while old ones
find new tricks to get you outside the door,
into the horror which is the one thing
you know for certain
awaits you there.

They say you loved them once.
Really? What was that?
Another trap, perhaps. You can't be up
to their devious ways. Keep
on your feet, ever vigilant,
go without sleep, don't eat,
forget you have physical needs,
you can't afford distractions now,
in this long battle, an attrition of wits,
between you and this sacred cow
they're calling duty.

Well, they have time
for such luxuries of mind. You,
of necessity, have left such inconsequential matters
long ago, well aside.

And still, on a dappled Easter Monday
it came that you loved me once.
We were standing on a small bridge
while the dog capered on the riverside.

Sic transit

For Margaret O'Grady &
Rachel McMillan Hall
Deptford, 1968-2003

When the wind swirled in the three contiguous
    courtyards
we had to run up the stairs closing three floors of
    casements.
Students would forget to shut them when they went
    out
and one or two of the panes would always come
    crashing down,
triangular shards exploding on the concrete-tiled
    ground.

A drunken girl fell from the roof one time,
slipped off a surface supposed to be out of bounds,
floated three storeys in the hours of the silent night,
cracked her pelvis in a hexagon of stone and shrubs
then crawled three flights back to her Tinkerbell cot.

We had police dogs, coke dealers, needles, walk-in
    theft,
allegations of indecent assault, scandal of every other
    sort
and budget cuts, the fabric of everything around
falling into inexorable decay; the sense that if there
    was a pits,
then this was it and we were sunk in it together.

No-one liked the place
or gave it credit for its smoke-bricked, airy grace,
its symmetry of threes, its sixties' spirit
or the visionary sisters who had built
the grade two-listed college next to it.

Yet I still dream of the house I had,
not as it was, inhabited by friends,
but with its roof taken off
and the sky-blue curtains I made
writhing like tortured souls
in the water-stained ruins.

Now there's nothing left,
a flimsy, high-rise, post-milennial palimpsest
perched on that tripod print.
And our survival humour, grim endurance,
spits and spots of joy and grief,
all unselfconscious, self-contained,
the whole of this now washed away,
without sentiment,
like Jeyes Fluid down the drain.

Pabellón del Espejo, Madrid*

There's a man and a woman behind me.
She's been left by her husband,
he's trying to convince her he understands
and how she must have a sensible, rational plan.
It's all wrapped up in cavalier expressions
of macho splendour.
He dismisses her doubt,
merely with the power of his voice.

The world as he sees it
is what he has deemed to it be,
not the other way round,
and she finds his vehemence, his warmth,
      reassuring.
He makes her feel how weak and fragile a woman is,
how, after all, she's being silly and,
though he's only a disinterested friend,
of course he must be right.

In the mirror his body tells different
but this she's unable to see
and when she goes home later tonight,
she'll feel the world all the emptier
because she'll know that she,
who observes the world first
then reaches her conclusions,
is, sadly and irrefutably,
though grieving,
entirely correct re her plight.

*a famous café in a mirrored pavilion

Arrest

For Tom

This black,
this beckoning void,
this pit of listlessness and despair,
this knife's edge of turmoil,
this wrenching gut,
this clamour of darkness,
incohate, incoordinate, blind,
this Loch Ness monster, conger-eel,
excrescence of sea-slime, wormwood, bile,
this anguish of sorrow, torture of grief,
this arson, this isolate fear,
this easing of spasm, this nearing-the-end,
this being-taken-by-surprise by the motioning hand,
this never-knowing-when,
this prostration,
this wretched, scalding brief,
this knowledge, this dawning,
this nascent, cool relief,
this inalienable certainty
this Godforsaken, awful ruse,
this iniquity of fate,
this truth.

Good Friday

'Morra Séamas!'
'Mine name isn't Séamas'.
The little boy scrunched his eyes,
anger somersaulting in the air.
It was Joseph
but my father didn't care.

He was a little boy himself once
and he liked baiting them
to see if they were capable,
as he had been,
of facing down a dare.

Mooghaun

i.m. Evelyn

An island paradise out of time,
this ring fort on a small hill in a cosy wood,
beyond lie other hills and compact lakes,
each with an ancient and traceable Gaelic name;
the estuary to the west, and the turret hill,
the re-modelled O'Brien castle below,
with its golf course, palatial bridal suites
and, deep inside, a portrait of Brian Boru.

Yet the stones from the concentric fort
are meshed in tree roots with the wrapping waste
shed by visitors at the viewpoint palisade:
cigarette foil, beer cans, bottles half full of lemonade–
where once were found torcs of gold
and awareness of the debt we each owe to the soil.

Insomnia 2

If you're not taken by surprise
the journey towards death begins with sleep
or lack of it.

In those long, dark hours of night
when a scratch becomes a ravine
and a breath of wind the jaws of Hell,
the rest of the world lies blissfully unaware
while you are accosted by unrelenting waves of fear.

The morning finds you isolated by leaden fatigue.
You know you've just imagined things
but have no purchase
on the humdrum day-to-day.

Sheringham

i.m. Mary

What it must be
to look out on a sea
that is not your own,
to work as a wife
in a house
that is not your home,
to surrender a child
you never have
and never will
know.

Carmen

i.m. Carmen Conde (1907-1996)

Fruit of the *Mar Menor*,
flat and a dark powder blue,
the open clasp of a secure embrace,
child of an unexpected birth,
and your own child, in turn,
impossible, born dead.
Your progeny in the years to come
all formed in the ferment
of your leonine, tempestuous head.
A cruel tax on one
who drank to the full
the sweaty pleasures
of the lovers' bed.

Mother of all those female poets in your wake,
firebrand, Catholic, and devotee of cats,
did anyone truly understand you?
Amanda, perhaps, but she died,
then you too paid that final, awful levy,
the descent into oblivion,
a living body with an exiled mind
in the wing-backed chair
of an old folk's home
somewhere to the north of the capital, Madrid.

Armistice (1918)

An armistice is almost a deadlock
but one side pays the price
and the other, though in ruins,
slaughtered millions on both sides,
retains what it thinks
is vindication and its pride.

In our case,
I cannot see beyond no-man's land
to the stationary carriage of negotiation,
nor hear across the silence.
I know hostilities are at an end
but not which one of us
will have endured capitulation.

Useless

Six years ago tomorrow
my mother's life-support
was switched off.

By her reckoning,
at least a week overdue.

Yet again,
she couldn't trust us,
when it came to it,
to do the job properly
on our own.

Long 3

In the arms of a dancer
my ship came ashore.
I've been at the captain's table
and promenaded on board.
I've gazed on the littoral
from out in the bay,
and bathed in the night stars
with anchors aweigh.

No.

The tunnels of darkness:
elongated toilet-roll hearts
through the long whitewash
of nights without sleep
and the pallid grind
of each waking day,
flatter to deceive.

The End

I mistook you for someone else.
Pardon me. If I had glimpsed you
from afar on the street
or been blinded by the sun
behind your face
or otherwise distracted,
any would have been an honourable excuse,
but mine was a full-knowledge mistake.

I greeted you head on,
the key to all my dreams –
and what a long time your coming
had seemed to take!
But I was wrong.
You were no more than a passer-by
who happened along
and acquiesced for a while,
out of curiosity,
a fish to a miscast fly,
a sinuous twist
of whose glistening tail
was all it took
to somersault
from off the hook,
open its fins
and scamper, joyous,
back to the burbling rocks.

The Heron on the Lake 2

There he was, or she,
large, grey, neck in chest,
bill extended like a handle
and perched on a timber stake
at the midpoint of a chain-linked fence
separating the boating expanse
from the little waterfall
at the top end
of the manufactured lake.

A heron, a decade on,
a decade older, perhaps,
keeping watch
like that distant relative
all that time ago
on the Binnenhof in the Hague.

This time I took a snap
on a gadget not thought of
a decade back or so
when I walked along that canal
in the peaceful, sky-filled
Netherlands.

Indeed, my mother always asked
what were the things
that we would see
when she was dead and gone.
This camera phone
we take for granted now
would certainly be one.

Mili-

For Elizabeth

Four blocks of butter is what you weighed
in a life-span amounting to two days.
Cradled in a palm of disparate, mourning hands,
locked together
by your skin, your nails, your veins, your ears, your
    hair,
your being briefly among them
and, unforeshadowed, taking leave
never to return –
exquisitely formed
then hobbled, for changeling grief.

Account Closed

                                              i.m. Josephine McNamara

Death will become her
as life certainly had,
though not in those last years
marooned on an island
of panic and alienation.

Debts owed:
to the beauty she would never
have claimed; to love, of which
she gave unstintingly; to duty,
by her children lovingly
returned; to wonder,
of which she always knew
the worth and always took
full measure.

Each now settled in full.
Account closed, no debit
accruing in the long
ledger columns of God.

The Old Home

In a time before instant communication
when we did not have a phone,
if his chauffeur brother was about to visit,
he would dream of it the nights before:
their childhood in the old home.

He never said it pierced him,
I never thought it did,
but my dreams of the house we lived in
are painful. They skewer me,
like heartburn, through the core.

Honeymoon

A couple of years short
of the half-century
they might have had
– had they come to an arrangement
a decade earlier,
lived a decade or so more –
we, their progeny,
entered Wynn's Hotel.

A staid place
of stodgy Sunday lunch
for extended families,
and broad-cheeked Czech waiters
not as much out of place
as might at first appear.
The same surroundings,
these days artfully preserved,
though ours are different times
from that first week long ago in Lent:
up from the country
in foreign Leinster
on a three-day *lune de miel*,
a name-only convert
(so his children would share the joke
when he scoffed, occasionally,
at the One, Holy, Apostolic Church),
a bride who would have taken
'one of them'.

That was nineteen hundred
and sixty two,
only seven years
before the first man
walked on the moon.

The Fit

You made it fit,
feel whole again,
you always do,
a special gift
of blending in,
of settling things,
the missing part
is always you.

Your time is short,
your visits rare,
another place
or face or time
will certainly
beguile you
into fascination,
some other where.

And yet,
such precedence
is always fleet,
it never satisfies,
for everything
you need
is here,
but nothing
you require.

Bloc

Never fear the blank page,
out of nothingness all must come
and back to it return.

Wait patiently in the void
and the message will be spun.

The Heron on the Lake 3

What have I seen of late?
That heron again, on the lake.

A tourist, I'm told
from a nearby heronry,
come regularly
or maybe several in their turn,
to occupy a place,
standing on one or other
of the many wooden stakes
across the lower part,
the stepping stones and
the mechanised cascade,
on the man-made lake.

A living bust, an oracle, a sphinx,
with the handle of a walking stick
for neck and beak.

Epilogue: Easter Saturday

A quarter arc of rainbow
shot across slate and slate-grey cloud,
the rain barrel at the eaves.
The Romanesque cut-stone gate
and the mossy, springy lawn
tucked round the graves
in the walled Church of Ireland enclave.
My ancestors here, servant with lord,
bound to a common obsolescence,
like the once sacerdotal trees
now shorn from the boundary stone,
and the genealogies and the mausolea
tugged by sleep towards the ground.

> *What matter? There's almost no-one here*
> *to mind them now.*

The next day,
the full arc, determinate
over the arch of a little stone bridge.
The green pasture, the low hills,
the pastel houses and the pattern of the fields,
moist yet fulminant,
with locals and livestock
absorbed in everyday deeds.
Some maybe at Mass
in hope of resurrection,
most indoors and oblivious,
beneath the wingspan of that silken prism
thrown across monochrome clouds.

And this humpback bridge?
So frustrating for modern convenience.
A technicolour rainbow with a fabled crock of gold?
Codswallop for tourists.
Cop on. Life is complicated.
And the telly has more wonders to behold.

Also by Jean Andrews

Poetry
In an Oubliette
Lunatica
Sí-Orphans of the Plaintive Air

Translations
Nancy Morejón, Black Woman and Other Poems
Carmen Conde, While the Men Are Dying
Eibhlín Dhubh Ní Chonaill, The Lament for Arthur O'Leary (in *Sí-Orphans*)

www.ingramcontent.com/pod-product-compliance
Lightning Source LLC
Chambersburg PA
CBHW071324040426
42444CB00009B/2077